I0079241

SHEARSMAN

DOUBLE ISSUE

85 & 86

WINTER 2010 / 2011

EDITED BY
TONY FRAZER

Shearsman magazine is published in the United Kingdom by
Shearsman Books Ltd
58 Velwell Road
Exeter EX4 4LD

www. shearsman.com

ISBN 978-1-84861-110-8
ISSN 0260-8049

Subscriptions and single copies:

Current subscriptions—covering two double-issues, each around 108 pages,
cost £13 in the UK, £16 for the rest of Europe (including the Republic of
Ireland), and £18 for the rest of the world Longer subscriptions may be had for
a proportionately higher payment, which insulates purchasers from
further price-rises during the term of the subscription.

Back issues from n° 63 onwards (uniform with this issue)—cost £8.50/$13.50
through trade channels. Single copies can be ordered for £8.50, post-free, direct
from the press, through the Shearsman online store, or from bookstores
in the UK and the USA.
Earlier issues, from 1 to 62, may be had for £3 each direct from the press,
where they are still available, but contact us for prices for a full, or partial, run.

Submissions

Shearsman operates a submissions-window system, whereby submissions are
only considered during the months of March and September, at which point
selections are made for the October and April issues respectively. Submissions
may be sent by mail or email, but email attachments—other than PDFs—are
not accepted. We aim to respond within 2–3 months of the window's closure.

CONTENTS

This House...

This house on a Greek hillside with its geckos and millipedes
wind bringing rain down from the mountains, the shutters
closed at night. Me with my mill-talk quieted, lying here
in the night and weather trying not to remember
trying to forget failed claims pains of inarticulation
and true attachments. I don't forget. I don't remember very well.

There were never any gods of rain, peasant of the elements
who gets on with the allotted task and washes the white stones
on the red path, slides them down the hill. That rushing sound.
That particular brow. Unerasable intimacy. Far from here
northern town cold night wet streets curtains closed glow
of radiator red in dark room, illuminating the hangings.

Anywhere, a coming together and making a voice, a god's work,
a voice for ever, a voice at large, in the mountain sides
the small mills in stream clefts turning their wheels at night, that
rushing, hollow sound. A double voice of solitude and connection
melancholy and ecstasy writes itself into channels of the earth
and dream between walls at night of distant points of contact.

This house on a Greek hillside with its geckos and millipedes
and painted walls. The vast wars raging across the earth
the law of the heavier weapon . . . When the heroes come we run
        and hide,
we peasant faces, irrelevant elements, we are lost and done for
and kick stones in the road, the dirt road that winds up
into the hills. Our sighs run back down the meadow.

The god's eyes looking suddenly up to us in the carved stone,
the warm air wafted up from the heater, stirring a few cobwebs
on the ceiling rose. Two fires signaling across Europe.
I'm twisting my voice out of its body to rescue a glimmer of
       recognition
from the blasts of warfare. I'm working hard at this:
I'm not singing and not shouting. I'm looking for a stone.

All the pebbles I've picked up from all the desolate shorelines of
       Europe,
a worn grey stone with a straight white line across it from Denmark
I press this stone into the world body, the dark mass,
to make there a small silence, in which we can hear
the faint sounds the insects make, the grasses hissing in the wind
the unrepresented voices of the generations. In the hard edge

Of this sphere the dead also speak, massed seeds in flower heads,
and in this seeking to gain a recognition, to participate in a chorus
which strips me of sad particulars, and address the gods,
by stones, yellow flowers, CD players, anything that works and say
that in the orkestra my guilt will modulate into the collective.
Well it may, or some other voice while the sun
drives under the earth and we tune our voices to its echo.
Voices working together, for an honest peace, for sense
in the structure, for tangle threads that connect across the indigo.

palm

                                    when   thou   pass   est

                                    through   waters

a smooth trunk parts   the words
        fronds above
                                    I   will   be with

                                        thee

        at the rootless base

a thee tree   a three tree

                                    we held crosses believed
                                    to be palm

        crayon a body on this tight woven parch ment
            a limp doll
                                    cupped in a small

palm tree   an alien

fashion for a paved garden

        without branches to cross

pin   nate   pen   ed

6

                    through   palms

                    can   i   pass

St Michael's
8 December 08

pines

if the tallest pines
press close
find their places

who else is here
a plaintive cry
or just a calling cry

the base finds us
buttercups

cries of irritation
a clash of pebbles
they're saying piss off

sightless
slightnesses
some stupid arguments

home killed
signed on the butcher's van
s(laughter)

lower branches snapped
a telegraph pole
of broken rungs

the base is only the base
but it is
fox gloves

a patch of sand
flicks her ears
above the ferns

North Hill
3 June 09

boll

is that the way I write?

there is no way
or this is it
below the bole

you are going on
and may be coming back

your ears are susceptible
when I thought nothing was

I dreamt that the bowl
was not important

later it had disappeared
from the table

I touch wet base
word blur
hart's tongue

bark bulge
above my head
                a blown wall

but this is simply absorbed
no need for repair

the birds return
a flicker or a promise

you are standing still
ears exposed

hair marked
by lichen

the thinning skin
if it specks?
                if it speaks

North Hill
5 Dec 09

silver

candle lit with an IOU
the impot
        of the import

stone columns
upright in the light
cannot sustain

white flash of a tree
distortion from diamond panes

a series of stills
a film which consists of

constant movement in the branches

                                        silver birch
                                        dying at the top

                                        a gawky splay
                                        and still though louder

                                        the white butterfly climbs

                                        patches of grey near the base
                                        peel away

skin peeling is wrong

gated ~~communities~~
estates
are wrong

hello, he said
clinging to the pram
                    hello   lady
                        gor   geous

                              convolvulus has place here
                           is whiter than the skin of birch
                              gorgeous convolvulus

inside the cell
my credit flames

Julian's garden
8 August 09

Note-taking
Tout cela est matématique —Flaubert

A bit of heart falls away at the reader's
touch—perhaps a necessary
operating expense after coming so far

through soft rain on a Sunday afternoon
to find the answer is absent in a place
once crowded with strangers. A narrow street

passes endless windows to arrive
at the letterbox whose contours once crossed
the distance between your fingers. A pavement

singer with small hands and a strange
amalgam of narrative postures
fills the puddles with his reflections.

But there's nowhere for them to go, no way
to keep their borders safe when they dissolve,
except on this page, empty and waiting.

Waking
after Fernando Pessoa

from nowhere
this butterfly
on your sleeping temple

a breeze—the window opens
the faded poster of a princess
flutters on a peeling wall

this breathing
happens
it isn't yours or mine

perhaps in your dream
you face me in the flesh
without a plan to follow

no one will ever join me there
I shan't be able to leave
without crying

you open your eyes
not knowing why
and smile

you've left your dress
outside
in the slow and wavy rain

Shifting registers

It's always the same train that can be seen
rushing forward with us inside trying to leave
our selves behind. Their eyes are those
we once shared, and there's something tricklike

about the new, as if nothing had actually changed.
It's we who are the intruders here, shining silvery
like semen on a sheet, spilt onto a geography
of rumples and older stains. Dead tired

we return along the dotted lines, the tunnels which lead
almost to a whole scene, though it takes a while
to recognise each figure and the just visible
colour of hair and eye. And though the whistle

of the train is still relevant, one of us is crying,
looking back through the window, where nothing now
intercepts our view of the distant city, whose perimeters
and dark rooms we once graced as tenants.

MARY LEADER

Codeine Sutra

Via the crooked portcullis, dawn enters, festering.
In other words, staples have been removed from the slit on

My inside left wrist. My right eyelid twitches realistically.
Festering in other words, staples have been suspended.

Razorblade, lightweight as sea foam; my right eyelid twitches
Realistically, On my left palm underneath the chart / chant

Of suspended razorblade. Light, weight as sea foam. Blue / red
/ Blue does not make pictures of melody on my left palm.

Underneath the chart, chant of. Suspended as soon as a
Diversion finishes, blue-red blue does not make pictures

Of melody. A line in the light of a flashlight as
Then; suspended as soon. As a diversion finishes,

As function is felt to have pooled the undone, a line in
The light of a flashlight. As, then, what, exactly, does it

Denote to describe, as function, is felt to have pooled the
Undone? A membrane, as fluid mosaic, suspended.

What exactly does it denote to describe in transit
To the hospital, tiger speed? A membrane as fluid

Mosaic suspended, measured in towels of green / red / green.
Six a.m. In transit to the hospital tiger speed.

Eastern Daylight Time. What is the roof of measured in towels,
Of green, red, green, 6, a., m., the bank, O a purple tree-

15

Shape within eastern daylight? Time? What is the roof of a
A gas station within a sky above facing the bank? O.

A purple tree / shape within at an angle of three fourths, say
Never! A gas station within a sky above. Facing

The profile in starlight as it haunts, at an angle of
3/4ths, say. Never the Robe of Night (on my lower left

Bedpost) profile in starlight as it haunts transparencies
Instead of. Boat-sound swells the robe. Of night on my lower

—Left bedpost, a cat combs in gray and quiet to the world,
Transparencies; instead of boat, sound swells, removed from the

Slit on my inside left wrist. A cat combs in gray and quiet
To the world via the crooked portcullis. Dawn enters.

Male and Female Seated on Whirling Logs at Water-Meeting~Place

Were beautiful and shone
Grew and were useful
The female and male beings
Made from stars like the grass

Mendel used paintbrushes
Of artists to transfer pollen
Intense prolonged alone
—Praise for the rainbow deity

Male Female Red White
Pink Grass Star Whirling X
Xs and Ys each part untiring
Mendel of the four peas

Mendel who tripped over vines
He of the egg-spattered pocket
Mendel whose eyes shone
She of the useful whole thing

White E

```
E e e e e e e e e e e e e e e O e e e e e e e e e e e e e e I
e A e e e e e e e e e e e e e T e e e e e e e e e e e e T e
e e C e e e e e e e e e e e I N e e e e e e e e e e e e S e e
e e e H e e e e e e e e e e e e e e e e e e e e e e e e e e e
e e e e e e e e e e e e e e e H e e e e e e e e e e N e e e e
e e e e e I e e e e e e e e e C e e e e e e e e e E e e e e e
e e e e e e N e e e e e e e A e e e e e e e e X e e e e e e
e e e e e e e T e e e e e e E e e e e e e e T e e e e e e e
e e e e e e e e O e e e e e e e e e e e e e e e e e e e e e
e e e e e e e e e e e e e e T e e e e E e e e e e e e e e e
e e e e e e e e e e I e e e X e e e A e e e e e e e e e e
e e e e e e e e e e e T e e E e e C e e e e e e e e e e e
e e e e e e e e e e e e e S e N e H e e e e e e e e e e e e
e e e e e e e e e e e                 e e e e e e e e e e e
e e e e e e e e e e e       e e e e e e e e e e e e e e e e
e e e e e e e e e e e       e e e e e e e e e e e e e e e e
T X E N S T I O T N I           e e e I N T O I T S N E X T
e e e e e e e e e e e       e e e e e e e e e e e e e e e e
e e e e e e e e e e e       e e e e e e e e e e e e e e e e
e e e e e e e e e e e                 e e e e e e e e e e e
e e e e e e e e e e e e H e N e I e e e e e e e e e e e
e e e e e e e e e e e C e e E e e N e e e e e e e e e e e
e e e e e e e e e e A e e e X e e e T e e e e e e e e e e
e e e e e e e e e E e e e e T e e e e O e e e e e e e e e
e e e e e e e e e e e e e e e e e e e e e e e e e e e e e
e e e e e e e T e e e e e e E e e e e e e I e e e e e e
e e e e e X e e e e e e e e A e e e e e e e T e e e e e
e e e e e E e e e e e e e e C e e e e e e e S e e e e e
e e e e N e e e e e e e e e H e e e e e e e e e e e e e
e e e e e e e e e e e e e e I e e e e e e e e e N e e e
e e S e e e e e e e e e e e I e e e e e e e e e e E e e
e T e e e e e e e e e e e e N e e e e e e e e e e e X e
I e e e e e e e e e e e e O T e e e e e e e e e e e e T
```

CHRISTOPHER MIDDLETON

During the Aftermath

1

Some Germans must have had a nicer attitude to death
but in Flensburg was a sloping guillotine
in shape so like the slide
in a playground for the children—
headfirst down a bed of steel you slid
and at the bottom or close to it
the blade, timed perfectly for weight/velocity,
dropped . . . So like a slide
(with oiled, polished levers at the top
and a technician to calibrate the dials)
you had a little time remaining
to think they killed you not just for now
but for the better part of your lifetime.

2

That covey of brothers, the sergeant pilots
of 16th Fighter Squadron, flew Tempests
and got up to no end of mischief:

one of the dances we went to
was held in the fumigated
military sector of the death camp

Belsen: with their gin they sipped
some ink and quite soon after
gave big smiles to the girls they danced with.

3

December 24, 1945

Petit mal had me shuddering on the floor
of a corridor on the line toward Hamburg,
then at Wesel the train stopped, it was 3 a.m.

Told to disembark we flocked to a breakfast.
Now again I come to be the gaunt overcoated man
groping for old food in a garbage barrel.

That is how it is here, millions who deserve it
itch to live in freezing twilight one day more.
Dim lights were on again when the train finally

rolled squeaking into the terminus. Piss
wherever you please, the police corporal shouted,
but put your bloody caps on straight now.

4

On the Königswinter ferry

A breeze from Aphrodite
lifting the hem of her dress,
war-orphaned Margarete,
her come-hither smile, soon
lips parted, Silesian lilt, our
(come together) silly whispers—
so, busy before conflict,
heavy in histories, merest
tokens in debate, some speech

rockets out of the mire;
and in a prelude ghostly,
allowing its wee bit of body
a brilliance, it lives
on a breath out of nowhere to name.

5

you were too numb to feel outrage
when Sepp your friend the Bavarian
Junkers pilot spoke of Poland as
the destination to arrive at bootlegging
cases of champagne. The sky-children
were too long gone to hear the silver
strings astir in hollow shells.

6

now vistas deepen, disappearing
behind the imaginable—to the nifty
organs of creation, to millions
of mutations in diet,
in soils, in sounds, in smells,
to the adaptations of an eyeball,
a beak, a skull, a lung

indifferent, culprits
in pain and yearning not at all
discovered satisfaction, stole
acutest pleasure
puffing on a cigarette;

if not exchanged, however,
for sprat or potato,
in its time a cigarette, rolled
from butts picked off the street, or shared
with that gracious old Pole who sketched us,
could only taste infected
like the language,
sour as the penitence.

7

Should civility to people be the practice?
Britain had wadded with plenty of sheepswool
the brains of her citizens in uniform:
the foreign past was simply not admissible.
Hide your life, by all means, but draw the line
at wasting it to placate brute power.
Some old sweats had certainly visited
cities in their splendour, waste lands now.
How flimsy they had been, how tawdry
the cheap guignol theatre of greatness;
hats and badges and strutting brigades,
all the folderol scared a supine people
into a funk deeper than ever before;
filth as never before had been their duty.
You could have known all this without feeling it.

8

Now catch a whiff of it,
Braunkohl, and bitter cold it is,
the smoke smells thick and sweet

of frozen Holstein villages,
their giant horses
with haunches the colour of rum,
of welcome
warmth in house and friendship.

Pass down this tunnel
under a mountain of burned bricks,
exchange words with desperadoes,
black marketeers
clutching their sacks
on salvaged pews.

9

was every day so crass, not for a moment
ever mysterious? Had a callus taken hold
to secure the soul for fellow feeling
but extracted from the feelings
some fibres of response? But then

one summer afternoon at a trot I passed—
not alabaster domes, silver spires, bright
pavilions disposed in avenues—a cabin,
solitary on the airfield perimeter,
a wooden cabin with a wonky porch
where wrinkled tobacco leaves

now seem to hang, no trellis,
no fabric for support, whispering,
not quite fragrant yet,
tenaciously from heaven to the earth.

10

by nineteen forty-seven anno domini
there had to be numerous capers,
their blessings like dandelion parachutes
for all of an instant prettified time,
yes, it was Warrant Officer Blow,
a round man and a wag with his badges,
also Fortune's toy but no fighter pilot,
who trotting back to his billet
from where our drinking was done,
slipped on a moonlit puddle and,
cavorting in that lunar pool,
could only rise again to fall,
so taking hold on the ankles of Blow,
laughing and capering we spun him,
blissfully unannoyed, on the double
pivot of bottom and moon.

11

You like her, don't you . . .
his pretty wife for a pound of butter—
him with his rosy face, too,
young as me, girl-wife winking . . .

I was not well enough acquainted with the cook
and to this day wonder how their cakes tasted
if that boy found a luckier man to please her.

12

Mnemósunë, dear one, salvage domina,
do not let those fractions
vex or be mistaken

("ripe, in fire dipped," said the book;
raise the pictures, they darken quickly)

or come closer, shadow
lingering in search of speech,
ready to pierce the poison-bag of trauma;
open to its boundary surely there is a place.

The spirit of evening loosened her hair.
Somebody did still fail to collect his wits.
Significant pattern entering all
behaviour that was old
being by incarnate evil dissipated,
as if on a day's march like any other,
into what pastures bleak did we then go.

*Echoes and allusions in four of these poems derive from Keats, Pound,
Wordsworth, Hölderlin, and Milton.*

Ô

while tones of planets descend
in scales as if thought were pitch
not picture but single note

while in the river's light spots
a train passing overhead
still in the rush of brakes you

while with tightening of the throat
air passes through zero cries
circumflex and guttural

while the moon's full of lost things
migrating birds unanswered
prayers keys emails of the dead

while re-engraved with its own
watered silk grainy surface
footage close up then far-off

while a body talking to
itself blood and nerves as sleep
rises through ears and water

while two heads crossed in the glass
a train passing from one ear
to another right to left

while this story's full of holes
in the edges of the space
you filled very slowly I

Wingprint

the colour of power hanging in the air
        is a word for sun on warm stone
made transparent

as sky and trees
      repeat leaves in flame
           on the other side a flight path

where finches throw their outlines
          wings etch themselves on windows

in the stun of what stops them
               an identified span
of feather grease and dust

               a curve of passageways
glazed over a bird
        flies in
           lost in exits
      and entrances   a tongue silent
          behind a mouth that moves through glass

when the door is locked it is alarmed
          somewhere between G4 and E7
or what I know and and how it's different from X

a restless wish for   what can't be googled
    and if so is it knowledge
             or the lost keys
that apple F won't retrieve

Variants on a Polish Fragment

After Julia Fiedorczuk

this is glass this is *szkła* or *szkło* depending on where
it catches the light and I can't see anything through it
only hear the rasp of broken bottles
swept across a beach where I'm walking
towards you with bare feet in this variant
salt air wears the edges smooth

words are sharp against the town's low roar
but blur your ears and traffic turns tidal every step
leaves a white wave of salt on my shoes
in *wody wielkie* in vast waters I could drown
in the undertow of any language
in this variant it would make no difference

if green's as green as *zieleń* I am walking through it
scent of cut grass on the rubbish tip
overhang of leaves dripping on the pavement
in this variant I'm spit and shadow ticking inches
over earth's impossible face this is how close I am
when shades of meaning grow luminous

in this variant I'm split in glass with one face
to the street and one tilted into planes where colours
fold back in silence the smell of rain
vanishes in the future there is no drizzle only
specks of scattered shine across a lens
in this variant you can't hear me coming

it's a city that asks questions, gives no answers

After Sigurbjörg Þrastardóttir

we may still cry in taxis
        though behind the window
it's not winter the electricity
        grids are humming
there has never been a word
        for crossfire in this language
shuffle the deck which one
        will you choose how will you
construct a house of cards
        so the stones won't fall
below the currency the city
        has thirteen hearts and none of them
is beating the circulation
        gone you play your hand
in this uncertain state
        it was not a heart attack
when he fell his ear
        pressed to the ground for
six-month-old information
        or digital toxic waste
grassed over the carbon cost
        of data cold enough to handle
she signs five times to say yes
        this is the whole truth all of it

In Search of Lost Time

I

After you've lost, searched, and come up empty,
you move on. For a long time I used to go to bed early
but the system clock is not accurate. You have
two options: one is to install timesynch software
but that won't hold for very long, so why not work on
punctuality yourself? I replaced the battery and that
seemed to do the trick. In all this gorgeous atmosphere
I dress in black every day, adding new features
where possible. Imagine having permanent jet lag
when legal professionals capture elusive billable time,
such as that spent giving reasons and dates, plus
sunrise and sunset in several hundred cities.

II

In real-time station departure I am unsuccessful in
retaining possession of the number of days, which do not
include the day of injury or day of return. No earlier
geared mechanism of any sort has ever been found:
it's always under construction, always under the burden
of unreliable data, but countdown clocks would show
how long this misery could last. A China lost in time
due to migraine symptoms swallows hours and hours.
Who can you turn to when times are flying out of joint?
Playing catch-up, she's fully engaged and ready to lead
the archaeological expedition that disappears and reawakens
elsewhere, the system behaving well during a finite period.

III

He would suddenly become aware that he could not
remember even time-lapse cameras recording glaciers.
A reasonable attempt will be made to replace time lost
but there is no magic form. Ask your doctor to complete
a press release pertaining to cloud estimates after earthquakes.
How can one hold joy and grief in the mind at the same time?
Blame advertising slowdown, or the growing literature
on the economics of migraine. Little is known about
why subjective time loss occurs after a novel experience
but mice allowed to sleep after being trained help you
shed flab in a jiffy. Between accident and absence
the world had changed into something unrecognizable.

Maxims, Minims, Squibs and Essayettes

1. By the age of forty—after a few years of practice—I'd learnt how to live the life of a thirty year old; but the time had passed, and my experience was now obsolete. And I started to realize that this would be true whatever new age group I was entering. So I began at last to comprehend the bewilderment on the faces of sane old people, marooned not only in a new era they knew little about, but a new stage in their own lives they had no experience of. And that much of the experience they had accumulated over the years was now irrelevant to them.

2. We are all children, even the oldest of us; children who will never grow up.

3. Comes a time in late childhood when the young lad knows it all, and has a complete and mature understanding of life, above his cowering juniors. Then puberty, and a shaking up of the hormonal glands, and the spectacular rise of Venus from the waves, and a new set of dilemmas not envisaged in the lad's premature maturity. And he becomes a little boy again, in adolescence's childhood.

4. And I know how the time stretches from their deaths, now. So, four days since Cid died, six years with my mother, eight with my brother. And I'm aware of them all—all receding. And how Cid's death *will* recede too, retreating further and further into the distance, more and more away from us.

5. As La Roche says, we assume that we will live for ever—though we "know" rationally we won't. And there is a certain level of awareness, which seems physically situated in us, that is immortal, and is neither an aged man, a youth, a "mature" adult, nor a child. No doubt it dies when we do, but it is easy to imagine it being unaffected even by that.

6. Death doesn't round things off. All its relationships are rent jagged-edged through the middle.

7. A small section of the congregation, or populace, will take the revered God or idea seriously, and ask "What is God?", "What is Freedom?", "How do I stand in relation to God or Freedom?" And maybe beat their heads against the wall to bludgeon the Truth in. But for most people going to Church is a social event—and you kneel when the Sanctuary bell rings, and stand to sing "Faith of our Fathers" after the "Ite missa est"—whatever the faith of your fathers would have been.

8. You see a spider, which also notices you spotting it. And the motionlessness is tense, visible—almost as visible as the scuttling-off would have been (though it's in you, too). Similar to the silence of a person asked an awkward question about somebody else, when the silence falls audibly, and the answer is indicated unquestionably by the silence itself.

9. "To face whatever is." I have some sympathy for this objective. But it is by no means clear what is; and if it seems to be clear, that is not because it has been discovered, but because it has been pre-supposed.

10. Rain on the hills, cloud fringe smudging into the valleys—with grey mountain wall behind.

11. As for "Eternity", timelessness rather than endless tine was what people had in mind. Does "I saw eternity the other night" raise the question: and how long did you see it? For the instant of a lightning flash. Or in Vaughan's case, a sinking into the timelessness of the stars.

12. A nostalgia, much more poignant, for those events that never did occur.

13. They talk about the energy of youth—and it's true. But there is also a divine lassitude you have then stretching to infinity, that you never have again, all too aware, later, of the brevity of life, and the rapidity of its decades, and how little time will any longer become available to be squandered on such ecstasy.

14. ". . . be devious, as my mother always said." (John Phillips) Women are pretty skilful at being either devious or direct—as they choose, and as you don't choose, and as they choose you don't choose. It was very kind of his mother to get him up to speed on this. *My* mother believed I should be completely entangled in women's wiles, and that that was the correct thing for a man to do—to be undone.*

15. We're on parole from somewhere; and if we break certain unknown conditions of our parole, will be recommitted to whatever detention centre we've been released from.

16. It's funny how we sometimes slip into our past, almost as if it were unfinished business.

There is a grain of truth in this, but mostly it's unfair to my mother.

Why

Because
he sweet-talks her in places she doesn't want to be where her fingertips
turn bloodless from the rhythmic pushing motions with her hands away
away
because
the tea he serves are wills and wonts she never hears him breathe at night
beside him her dreams are tumbleweed and tell her *I am only one* over
and over
because
she chews time he hangs her love out to dry and oil paint takes
a minimum of thirty years to dry she can never remember exactly this
dream
because
she has read somewhere six new planets orbit a star five in a liveable
zone only
they are light years from earth and already what we love is time they
spent is slipping
because
why is for Wyoming and weather and cross-eyed it is weightless
and welcome
and also for wasp and for where
because
their love is finding a view she is sick of this small miracle under the clouds
where he gets in her hair cajoles her outdoes her outwits her
because
she may be an orange peeling itself under a desert sun
when he can't get over *how beautiful yellow is!*

To The Highest Bidder

A clearance sale to do
oh Christ
away with everything
including him including her.

Including the space across the table at which they met.
The bike ride that final day of autumn.
The crystal scream hand-blown
with the maker's initials etched in.

Including also the bones he had to pick with her
the unwanted gesture of abandonment
a raised hand open like stone
a take-away heart
furry
probably German
probably belonged to one of them as a child.

Also to go under the hammer:
a telephone in mint condition with all the words still in.

A bitter fish the bitter lemon.
A leaking teapot
the colour yellow.

All rubbish
all he
all of it she.
All of it bubble-wrapped.

We are also there seated among the bidders.
Consider what we might take
what we might use.
What then might be ours.

once more

everything comes from it and returns to it

even elastic bands breathe slowly in and out feign
sleep feign like a bat hung on dusk she listens
to his breathing in and out of what she longs for
the letters of her name ~~unzipping once more~~ even
elastic bands dissectare slower than paper than he lets
slip the dark once more she lies ~~on he and she~~ touching
her waiting beside him once more ropes of the night
very slowly the ropes of night tighten once more beside
her the man ~~lies the man beside her lies~~ the silence
~~lies she~~ was she the silence even elastic bands yearn
the sheets between he and her conceal the man sinks
his chin sinks the silence in the pillow and further beyond
his breathing ~~forehead his jaw~~ his body falls once more
about what his dream—not ask falls his dream
once more she reads blackberry bushes on the ceiling

once more once more her breath searching
for his buttocks his back his hand
once more she

may she once more?

turn around you
turn around.

The light switch

On the west coast of Canada
a human hand has washed ashore.
It's the sixth case in eleven months

and the second in under forty-eight hours.
The sixth hand is a right hand just like
the first four hands. The fifth hand, found

on a Monday, was the first left hand. The third
hand was found near the second. It's as yet unclear
if the fifth hand pairs with any of the right hands.

It remains a mystery who the six human
hands belong to.
Not to the same person—that's for sure.

No hat
no boots
no job

What to do? Little else to do.
Read the news, masturbate,
watch a documentary on TV.

No, not on the world food crisis.
That's old hat old boots no job:
the most expensive hotel in the world.

No, some asylum seeker
after some twenty-three years
returns to Romania where,

the people speak a language
in which
practically everything rhymes.

After the commercial break, his
(the Romanian's) hand presses against
the old front door and then (and this amazes me):

his hand infallibly slides round the doorframe
and blindly insinuates
it's way clear of the vigilant walls

with the self-assurance of a back pocket
and the brevity of life stuffed deep inside.
Like

someone who has been far away from home
for a long time can still find the light switch.
Instantly. Like someone.

Manqué

A manqueller gestures at   *abuser*
a woman of great weight.

Mandarins nod all
through the train. Mandatory

papers fly from deep
pockets while manciples   *bondslaves*

manichees maniculls   *third century sectarians, sons*
mandrakes pay mancus   *human-shaped roots, thirty pence pieces*

for manbotes and one rich   *fines for the loss of men*
boy searches baggage

for his mislaid passport
in his good time.

Transmutation
in the John Rylands library

My stacks are iron, too. If I could tell
the difference between writing and reading

and raise the temperature till I converted
each to each, my exemplars would buckle,

words burst hot like fat crystals
on a mountain of marrow.

Tattoo on the Heart

We go beat pace.
She won't gallop
though I plan
to break my neck.

She could race me
but, in inching,
hopes to over-
run. Our death's

my decision.
Since my differ-
entiation,
I am sore,

itching. Tiptoe,
we go foal ways.
Bandages of
thought will come

off. In mud-blood—
mixed in our con-
taminated
artery—

you will see a
perfect image
of her mind,
her mine, on me.

Call Up

in Burghclere Chapel, Hampshire

If such a place were of no blood,
its people plump and clean,
its things pure as fresh
sheets, new cushions, light
downless quilts, dugouts
dry slits in the ground,
barbed wire harmless
hair tied with silk,

I'd go to the great houses
crowded in a camp
and not find ugly
ruins nor inhabitants
eating wild higsbane
nor traitors swallowed
by the square-toothed devil.
I wouldn't see legs
dangle from crook of lip.

When I arrived there
kitbag across my shoulder,
I'd lay out my trivia,
arms on a blanket,
tortoises to stroke, tiny
crosses by the hundred.

TOM LOWENSTEIN

from Ash Farm Journal

The following journal passages are extracted from a long and unfinished prose poem whose narrator, the previous afternoon had written Kubla Khan. *The context is the farm house where Coleridge putatively wrote his celebrated poem. I have made no attempt, beyond references to Purchas, at writing literary history.*

Hic labor, ille domus et inextricabilis error — Aeneid. VI :27

An apple tree. The full, charged, fructified, complete effusion from itself, perfect in self-generating abundance, a variegated expression of what it stands through the summer to carry into October. And so it raises its progeny to the air, and these hang in beauty, passive in allowance of the wasp, ant, tit mouse and the small red mite that crawls its mossy ridges. An apple tree in fruit is nature's noblest expression. The weight and colour of this harvest: 'autumn's foison big with rich increase' (Sonnet 94?)[1] hung from a living and supple wood. I've seen bramble and blackthorn loaded with dark berries. But the apple is our richest inheritance. One bite of it, moreover, from our first parents is engraved in each human brain. But much as I glory in this fruit, just two, if I consumed them, would throw me in a colic.

*

This was mankind's primal ill. Ingesting not one apple: but the entire fruit tree. Indeed, the world's an orchard: rind, seed and core, that germinated in the hearts of our first parents and took root therein. It's these seeds in the head I feel ripening, corrupting me somehow. The roots grapple in my physiology. I feed this tree. It fortifies itself in me.

*

It was of course the *quince* that suggested itself, thrust forward in the primal orchard. How it glowed in the first hand that lifted it to become a pulp in the mouth. *Curious insinuation . . .*

---

[1] Misquoted from Sonnet 97

*

Golden and dry. And if parched, radiating precious creative light. Here the damp, organic interior expresses itself in a water-titrated green. The granulations of rock with their pittances of lichenous growth, ferns rising to knee height, and on the cliffs sea pinks in dry tufts, giving the lie to my earlier supposition of damp. But to return: even the dry grasses of the coombe have wetness flowing from them, as though melted from earth. This paradox I love. Perhaps I *cannot* love without such contradiction, for to be drawn and repelled in oscillating movement signifies the elasticity of natural and human relations. If I were drawn without remission, I would fear suffocation by attachment: thrown against what I willingly embrace until the organism ceased to breathe.

*

Say the word 'journey', and I reply *vicissitude*. Wet feet, weak boots and cold wind on the waistcoat. This volume of Purchas: it is ten pounds in weight. The burden of its information weighs equally on intellect and body.

*

A fool marching along the way marked his passage of return by the disposition of sheep on the hillside. He turned home in the evening and the sheep had been frozen into the postures and pattern in which he had earlier found them. 'This can not be,' said the traveller in his folly, and plunged into the woods where he lost himself for ever.

*

This fable occurred to me as I missed my way thro' Culbone Wood and became lost, so I thought, to extinction, in the long, dark, steep chasm that leads, at last, into the farm precincts. It is a *romantick* wilderness in which to divagate. It is thunderous with stream water and somewhat threateningly enclosed with trees which have thrust their canopies almost preternaturally high in their effort to transcend the abyss whose darkness they themselves have created. The ascent is very steep, strewn with cumbersome limestone rocks, and there being no clear track, I was driven to stumble in a zig-zag and meander, now across the stream (and thus more than once submerging my boots), now over and sometimes beneath wild, creeper-shrouded heaps of fallen old tree-trunks; and on one occasion having to tear away a curtain of ivy, wild clematis and a lichenous green hanging whose smell I recognised but whose identity I could not recall.

Looking down through the forest—I was there an hour or more—the sea was distinct here and there through trunks, underwood and foliage. The water very level, grey and dead (or as if dying), as though October, which was occupied in ministering to leaf and flower, had worked also on the sea, which was sometimes pitted like metal which has been hammered, now pewter-coloured and now, as though soured, like a tarnished flat-iron. Fatigued as I was and near done in with the flux of a dysentery, I arrived in a sorry frame and needs must beg the necessity of a lodging and hot water. Here that night I consumed a medicinal draft of opium which stopped my bowel but was an aperiative to the imagination: highly coloured in experience, albeit vague, obscure, remote and fugitive to recollection.

*

Overcast sky as in the mind. As though the interior of the skull weighed down close and would rain. If thunder would only break. A positive mental release. Could I weigh my thoughts they would out-*scale* Purchas.

*

The wooded headland and the marsh present a quasi-spiritual mood. Dark green; purple. The wetness occasions a *descent*. By this I mean a *katabasis*, a *nekuia* from the unsatisfactory upper world to that nether realm of dreams and mythologies, haunted albeit with ghosts that reproach us.

*

Dead trees in a scattered semi-circle, each topped—as if with one dark, final thought—by a crow or rook. Lazily, they lift off and hop from one tree-top to the next. Thus thought, itself, langorously, and by association, moves without formulated pattern. The trees are as if earth had disgorged some ancient animal whose skeleton stands now exposed.

*

I carry two sheets of writing. While my ink horn, from which lines of verse must otherwise have emerged, remains full. The ink brims still in an undiscriminated mass, with a potency which it might have lent to the production of characters on the page, but impotent now to discharge its function. Somewhere in this liquid, my poem still lies unfinished: the Great Khan with his beasts and concubines walk peacefully there, undisturbed and undisclosed by my burrowing and (now) sleepless quill.

*

Smoke rises from croft signifying evening, repose and quiet industry. Shall I envy unpretending cottagers whose sole scope is these coombes and marshes, and whose phantasy lies in the imagining—from just one, albeit enormous source—of scripture? But then, just how do we conceive the figures who enact Gospel verses? Last month as I took my rest after work in the garden, all that arose against the inner eye were the leaves, stalks and flowers at whose level I had laboured. Everything against the coruscating black and inner eye was vegetable and weedy; small stones, even, had the scent of earth on them—and this also in the mind's eye! That the closed eye might in imagination detect a smell I attribute to that awakening of the senses which follows exertion. So in the croft, as the shepherd stretches his limbs by the fire and his goodwife returns from the labour of carding, they must half shut their eyes and enjoy the sensual intermingling of impressions that the day presented. Still, I am preoccupied with the question of how ancient figures, imperfectly represented in translation from some antique language, may come alive to present apprehension. The painting of Michelangelo is one thing. The quotidian reality—smells, forms, textures, gestures and inherited physiognomies—lie beyond intellection. If sacred life means anything, it has nothing to do with the drama of those remote eventualities—which is uninterpretable. What chance then, for croft-folk's apprehension . . . ?

*

On an earlier subject: plants that seed and take root in rock. Just as we who inhabit cities strive to live naturally among stone buildings and between walls.

*

Arches stretching heavily across the narrow path through the trees. Thick in stone and brickwork, rising from the bank with its brambles and ivy groping into the masonry. A strange and dark Virgilian architecture—as though at Cumae—and oppressive to the spirits—down to a gloomy bay whose languid water is just audible through the woods. Chestnut, holly, turkey oak and beech tumble abruptly from the path and are filled with the waste of ruined old trunks that have been thrown down across the arches which they (the tree trunks) appear sometime to have abraded. These arches have their sullen, quadrilateral bases in the under-wood, but they appear to come from nowhere at all and to have no other function but, it would seem, to brace the path at irregular intervals and offer the illusion of a gateway or threshold—beyond which there is just further pathway leading further onward to a destination obscured by trees and the heavy light that these enclose in a perpetual evening.

*

The present overtakes the past, but this colours it from below, shining vaguely up into what is being known and learned. As for the future, this is a white sea, a transparent supposition which has mental existence only. We anchor (here) at our peril in this ocean of irrealities.

*

47

The minor voices of the household. Kitchen pans, the rattle of a knife and spoons ringing in a dish which has now been emptied. What happens between hearth and table.

A boy runs in crying, 'Father, the black sow is . . .' his voice is lost now in the movement of a chair and the sudden run of boots. All this reaches my intelligence as it were through the tragic (!) medium of my intestine, which inhabits my body like a thick branch of ivy, convulsing and grasping at what it touches.

Earlier I imagined this organ to have been inhabited or possessed by the Tree of Life *ipse*. Could it be that this, even in the Paradise of the world's body, was sick already or even that this same tree was in itself a *parasite* of Paradise?

If the serpent was its inhabitant—its presiding spirit indeed—a component aspect of its life-sap dwelling both in its trunk and branches and internally within the sapiency of its grain—moreover if that the serpent was the writhing and energetic force of the tree: *its* poison was perhaps the apple's savour... a feverish sweetness which offers the taster no respite from an overwhelming number of desires. (The flavour of life, as elsewhere I have suggested, being what that first bite left in the mouth and which is inheritied by all the sons of Eve & HER SERPENT LOVER!)

For he, or that, which seduced her to consume the apple was her concubine—an epicene and semi-formless phantasmagoria—He (the snake) must have also entered ADAM: that man who was an emblem (diagrammed succinctly in three Hebrew characters) of earth in Persia—and in concert, consummated their initiation—a consumption of and assault on knowledge.

The black pig, meanwhile, which had been rummaging for a cabbage stalk that lodged behind the wicket, had thrust in its head and got stuck inside the sheepfold. She was dragged screaming to her quarters. They will cut her throat tomorrow morning.

*

This solitude—it is a compound of the silence which itself is an expression of space. This place is high, bare and remote. The sea is visible as a distant glaze, but the sky is closer and could be audible if the air arrived in rising wave-like movements that were checked entirely by trees, stone barns and hedgerows. The wind, however, travels through, leaving as its residue merely shreds and whistles, the tatters of an invisible fabric - a music to which the violin, the serpent (!) and bassoon do not aspire. All this then drops away leaving the house in peace and with nothing between the mind and infinitude but the mind's own restless, time-tramelled lucubration. I have made a practice of putting aside these perturbations (turbid/turbulence— the current of hot rock that is a psychic Phlegethon!) and then what silence: the soundless first moment before time and Paradise. Even before God, I was about to write, but must remember, as the Bible in this parlour reminds, that before God, there was Chaos—*tohu va bohu*. Or that rather God must have existed before and/or with or as a part of Chaos: that He was integral to that instability, flew, as it were, within it and then from those buffetings and tides, created the natural order, through which He continued flying for as the Hebrew saith, '*ruach elohim merachephet al p'nei ha ma'im*'. (The wind, or breath of God moved on the face of the waters.) And thus I imagine the first moment no longer as a silence. But that from the creative struggle (for that must have been a war with chaos), from the tension and engulphings of those contrary forces, came the 'second' first moment. Is there not peace in the following assertion: God created the Heavens and the earth. From this flows the silence in which, albeit temporarily, I have been settled. As a primrose in the hedgerow rises on its stem, the flower opens, and there it stands up modestly in crowds of weeds and grasses. This is the silence in which all things endogenously exist and co-exist. The relation between an object and its environment is mediated in silence and by it. The after-product of sound is extrinsic—it is something else. And since all sound arises from silence and returns thereto, it may be said that sound, quintessentially, is silence also. Out of the window—I look up from this page—I see the hawthorn hedge and a steep coombe with (further up) more hedge, thistle patches, sheep scattered across the meadow—and it is silence that I *observe*. Silence visible. I witness it in the sky, a stone, the path leading around this farm. The body produces its breath and some mucilaginous interruptions. They too are silence and fall back there. Patience! And waiting. Herr Goethe has written: 'Die Voeglein schweigen im Walde. Warte nur. Ruhe du auch!' These words, the very ink that crafts and encrusts the relation between vowels, consonants and diphthongs, *give me pause*. For they conclude a large proclamation in six brief lines which draws trees, mountains and the birds that live and sing in this wild cosmos, leaving the 'stage' of that imaginative geste empty. Through these lines we have journeyed through all Nature, then are left to the quiet of our proper selves to meditate in a silence which is a summation of the Great All.

*

If all journeys were inscribed on *mappa mundi*, the world would appear a dark, confused and trackless chaos.

*

Reverting to my Purchas. Here is a single volume containing countless thousands of voyages & divagations. And yet I can may carry this compendium along the country track of my own small human *aberration*. Narrative is a voyaging through *error*. Virgil expresses this (as I have quoted him already). There is no more sublime vision.

*

Are we essentially just onlookers to the *pictures* of things and the things themselves lie beyond the grasp of our senses? In imagination I have exgavated through the body of the lark and the primrose, the foxglove and the bramble and have arrived at a subtle and refined nothing. In itself beautiful, but too elemental to grasp with intellection or retain in memory. These essences co-exist with us and are within us but it is a work lying beyond work as we outwardly know it to travel there, dwell and return to the coarse outer integument.

*

Another small animal crushed on the bridleway. This time unidentifiable. Reduced to crude physical constituents whose most delicate formation, internal inter-connections and relations with its circumstance and environment had made perfect. Now a (perfected!) encrustation of rubbish. A rat possibly.

*

Pine wood on the ridge. As though giving my confused gait a *marching* order. I can not (always) avoid this.

*

The stream is a ribald and chattering bawd. It has intercourse with everything on its way. Thus I have admiration for this cheerful gutter. Then of a sudden an opening of the pasture, and the bay unfolds. Vast, grey-blue, peaceful, remote, mutable and treacherous. It takes effort not to love this more than the abject mud hole into which my boot plunged just now—wetly.

*

Sticks on the path in the pattern of the letter A. *Aleph . . . alpha*— from which *beth* flows nearly, and from there the entire current of concurrent alphabetical discourse on which we feed and depend (yes, also hang), and to which we nesciently contribute our progressive alternations. How much more simple to halt at the letter A. But even A is not silent entirely. Nor does it ever finish. For everything is contained therein.

*

Hawthorne tree battered from the north by salt winds rising from the bay and from the high coombe. Drier, and perhaps warmed, by its passage over flocks of sheep!!

*

The shepherd who recited to me his sister's own verses. She had written these perhaps at her school. The circumstance immaterial. He spoke them with admiration and sincerity. There is more learning and religious truth here than in many an academy or office of divinity.

*

The little blue scabious : stunted at the foot of a hedge, all the more intensely blue for its obscurity. I would almost repeat this for the sea aster which crowds the marshes at Porlock Quay. But abundance there creates instead enormous and flagrant glory.

*

To be in a hurry is miss almost everything. And arrival? The object has become invisible.

*

Nature is my cradle. And at every moment she rocks me gently and wisely towards my extinction.

LINDA BLACK

as pellets pool

& splatter   drip

in the ear   of transfiguration

mellow & melancholy

& roots are bared   & the spade—the heart

declines to split

in the hush and lull   amidst

the imprecision   the head

ringing like a bell   then the trees

will sway & billow & bend

& the Russian Vine   will wander

not circumspect   like I

Expectance

entrances (her)   waves

from all directions   as if bells

were peeling   light

overcome with perfume   sweet

lover's touch   were there to be such a one   loft

of all yearning   becomes   becoming

discernible   *but it is so!*   as landscape

sleeps into darkness   seemingly

not quite there

if the journey

be a long one

a suitcase   must be sought

of vast proportions   the arduous task

of preparation   does not

come easy   not easy

begun   nor at all   latterly

could be called

disarray   though softly

imposed   folding/smoothing/pressing

down   similar in tonality   liquid

as thought   can be

added to   and added

In this land

Of living proportions

Accruement and dispersal what need

Of this amounting *seed-welt/wold-warp/spittle*

That gathering of the un-together

Each laden branch

Wilting *soul-slew/catch-curl /forbears/fever*

All of which is wounding

To the already wounded *cross-axe/hatch-bow/word-weld/dagger*

You ask how I know I speak

Of institutions failings of mores personalities

Whose props may (as well)

Be the dunces-cap the cane the wielding

Of liturgies *whip-gall/snake-lore/rebel*

And so on locking up repetition the culling

Of what could be *switch-block/bone-metal/ spindle-finger/meddle*

As we would have it as we thought

We knew it *nay not ne'er*

The composition of soil

its exhumation   its seepages

harbinger

of the wriggling   malleable

in its nature   in variations   & all its various

properties   the country over   wide

& deep-set   endless

in its constitution   wayward dense & undulating

slip-soil slow-soil sacred-soil   soft

ash and bone   embellished

in formation   foundation

of all that is natural   its defiance

of ever ending

*

through the window she *sees* the garden

sharp & forthright   earth-patch life-patch lease

of life — *sees* the ascending — *sees* the plum tree   birds accumulate   amongst its dead branches   source

of life   wall trellis pergola   urn

of earth   (down to)   athwart

in feign protection

Woods in Room

I

winter woods pull   a person's   figures in
amongst moss   -clothed tall ones   a step
on a crunch of broken solar   moments hear

ing is crisp readings of brown crack   ling
mouths shed   from intricate plays all   sea
sons lose to tongues   of ice & wind's ever

-elongating signature passing through sens
itive   branches to   pick up bits   of twig
&   bark brambles   are agreements feet can

not accept where trousers may   rip against as
one who is lonely pulls   their mouth of open
tasting through rough closed   slats & cross

-hatch a smell   of wood-mould &   mush
room shapes an asocial gath   ering in some
human nostril a   thrush blurs   to crooked

      & twig   gy()re   minders

II

a lit   standing lamp & its   corner hold
dry gold liquid of passing stories & the
creek of beams that could become people

if the   one in   the room thought through
rings   & grain toes on wo   ven animal
hair feel traces of   travel placed   a bed

stead   is a crane that will   lift the heaviest
dream from the hole   of a human mouth
and the pillows are bags of old forgotten skills

builders zipped into each   feather two eyes
stare at three cracks meeting   on a ceiling
and passing away across the vast loss of a

ceiling's so   lid abyss it is   only the door
& its   pockets of knowledge & its   two
sides one warm the other   cold that makes

nothing an offering

III

win   ter woods pull at a standing-
lamp man figures   in amongst corn

ers of dry   golden li   quid moss
-clothed tall ones step on passing

stories'   creeks on the crunch of
broken beams that could be   come

solar moments hearing   people of The
one crisp reading(s) of   brown room

thought through rings crin   kling
mouths shed from g   rain toes woven

seasons lose animal   hair tongues
of ice & wind's t   ravel placed The

bed   crane is an ever   -long gate
-signature   passing through sensitive

branches will lift the heaviest dream
pick   up bits of bark   & twigs from

the hole of a   human pillows &
mouths in agreement with brambles

feet can't accept   old forgotten kills
trousers may rip   against built   zips

into   each as one who   is lone   ly
pulls their feather 2 eyes stare mouTh

open ta   sting through three cracks mee
ting rough closed slats & cross-hatch

ceiling passing away a smell   of wood
-mould in a vast loss of ceilings(') mush

rooms shape solid   abyss an a   social
gathering of doors in pockets of doubt

a human nostril & a Th   rush with its two
sides blurs   of twiggy reminder & oTher

cold make Thing a   No!   of fur & ring

Particular Winter, Trossachs, January 2010

Note: *Cruach Ardrain* is a mountain near Crainlarich, its name means – *stack of the high part.*

late light crumbles
across Coire Earb

Cruach Ardrain fades
and crisps and fades
and cr

isps as

snow-smoke surges
on gusts' tuning

spindrift-twisters hiss
grains of glint-sting
on my cheeks like

radio taking my skin
I am granular light like
this gra nular-lit-ground
could I & land be blown

away on wind
as frozen smoke

? drift-ridges & ice-clad
grasses scatter
light's fast passing
of pale gold powders

a   sheet

of   solid   lochan   holds
  shine   tight   on   ice   as
gauze   -spooks   of   snow

sheeesh   its   gloss
  a   moment

of   mountain   hare   fast
  as   a   statue   disintegrates
to   white   speed's

  furry   smoke   -light

"All these things I know from wandering the country"
(Lee Miller Dead child. Romania, 1938)

in a room where light fails
she lays out her child
binds him with string
to his coffin
begs him
not to return as a ghost

she puts a penny
in his mouth   and sings
an old Transylvanian lament
between phrases that entreat him
not to go   and phrases that beseech him
not to return

his sister leans out across the flowers
her bleached bare arm
reaching for the empty water jug
fleas have girded her waist and ankles
with rosettes of bites

Tracks

dull light and a cold wind—
we could be on the farm
bringing the cows in against a gale
through hock deep mud and horizontal rain

the copse is a grey smudge out across the field
we know the sharp lines there

the beeches grown tall   and we know
without looking that the rain

will be making its way in runnels and channels
down every twig and branch and the trees will be creaking
and looped below   arched and already rooting
the bare barbed brambles will be glazed with rain

Still Life

So since we cannot meet I'll put you here
in a small room looking out across the bay
your thoughts like water—just the ebb and flow
of colour and of light. The green, the grey

the luminously blue horizon
distant. What do you say to this,
drowned in a February sea? I give you light
and a safe room so you can speak to me

She takes Bone Monkey as a Lover

his yellow nails rake down her side
in welted lines that raise and grey
he loves me/loves me not she wails

he takes her out to eat and tells
the other diners she's so fat
says she's the one who worships him

he's brushed her hair until it flies
to flirt with his remaining strands
she hides the bruises   most of them

in bed he slides his narrow leg
between her thighs   he mounts her
as she sleeps and in her sleep she cries

he rocks her   rocks her   riding
all her dreams   he loves her
loves her not

Emblems from the Wolves

Bone Monkey swaggers through a plain of thorns
crowned with the insignia of warlike deeds—
emblems stolen from the wolves
are fixed securely to his skull with cords.

His war pipes are a swan's wing bones.
His headdress—raven, magpie, eagle, crow—
chitters behind him. Whispering as he goes,
he says "all I have dreamed is this

and now all I can dream is this".
Bundles of wormwood scour sun and moon
but nothing now is ever as it seemed.
As darkness grows

he lies down in a hollow in the hills
his tattered ribcage—a bowl of stars.

Richard Owens

Shepherds Lament

a good tree gives me shadow
pretty—behēoldon Þæt ͔ngel

koumfort wid she hann tek
de soffness—outwardly distant

tax-gatherers sent to scold
to meet & deal with us

messengers in their presence
embraced envoys—took stock

we were all very good friends
well disposed one to another

rapidly burning through reserves
for our part made no peace

having sewn such by such fed
quarterly losses—thence under

expected to match concessions
she stood turned to slip away

made me fast to assume cunning
tongue to the moving herd

now afield no longer standing
wræccan—with no hope of return

John the Revelator

an advocator—bot wi blude
bound for some
what shortly comes to pass

companion through affliction
as of a trumpet
who was detained among you

for their power is in the open
between hands
an indivisible wilderness

idol clothed in precious raiment
waiting in glory
a fire come on thee as a thief

a nakedness kept from the hour
come & see
deep in the rocks of mountains

that hath an ear let them hear
these against thee
world to rent—a living so bent

A Concise History of the Female

"But please don't cry— …
Beauty does not rest."
Anne Carson

What faith submits
my back a bridge for your feet
green ferns and day lilies over the pond
silver mirror and
inside the dark folds
smooth as stones,
the book
engages from suffering

Language unaccustomed from speech
malign me
I am not incremental
the flood as it imitates swallows
and I swallow but am not that
which is spoken of
grateful to be small
see the bodies as they float out to their graves
inside the tsunami

Her clitoris as it is cut out,
the light on the lintel as she is sewn
in the house of any village
sews my tongue
from the poem that breathes

In this urgency I speak to you, grieve,
make love—
the beautiful constellation of your brain
riding me into daybreak
a freedom past
unmanned bodies who have none, no sex left
have become liquid in the black dirt of a ditch
or only the words in my mouth,
speech through cotton

and I am somebody's wife but I am only
local
looking for my own
and I am no one's wife even
after ten years

Devotion does not ask for time,
the movements of trees and oceans.
What is gentle
the eye can answer without harm,
your hand on my back;
like fire in a metal can through the dark of night
on a city street—and homeless,
the new has been built

This darkness does not
will not be darkness as on Earth
we speak of the Sun, a god

and our orbit
one of isolation and fear
as if the coldness of space were itself cold, singular
and not just vacuum—
my hand outstretched in the winter air, chaffed

That which cannot be empty
I speak to
not divided but unremained
heat of stars and of energy
for there is nothing that protects us from passion
nor can there be
if we are to love like animals
beneath a Joshua Tree
and not eat each other
each limb chopped off and cooked for erasure

An excavation
two thousand years later reveals the bones
illuminated by yellow spotlights,
of Roman baths buried beneath a Medieval castle
in France,
each age consuming the previous,
then unearthed—
and would you not touch me
would you not love me if you could
decide
for humanity

Roots Surfacing Horizon, 3

Blindness of root visibly cradling the outsake on surface   exsurgence of difference minus departure, whole pillars of dependence are engrossed by thinnest plate   horizontal distillation invokes rebuttal at horizon

the series 'dwelling' cased down by pared horizon   disaster by tractable origin until refaced at trait of root fixed by exit rank   its own motile bluff off banksome exposure

what is 'unthought' in the flatness-decongestant ribs a stay through covering soil, sublimates inference as relational opacity rootal not neutral   the 'sub' behind this vertex versions a spell elational with surfacing, planar pull to an horizonal abrupt universal cell

> call of horizon
> no sooner discerned
> you do have the chosen
> noise on behalf of, its
> wanted prior standing

Each root fold is a relict of sky deposited on its coils of flathold   the elbow out at mimetic surface, not skin but root-trampled to where the horizon ramifies   an infill clinging to field hollow with horizon, letting the ancient hole usurped by aperture hold again

travel of roots thwarted above their element, re-admitted but on soil-gesticular terms: guard against any over-recognition of the called from its forth   horizon as extra transfer is webbed down but as projective greeting releases the plateau's self-guiding a whole leap out

the fronds of surface (distributive trust) become goads of plenty
branching out but only as nodal as horizon was   condensity of the
flat sheen surface population, what ripples is the transfer from every
other density

> lead a wad of surfaces
> true from such depeelings
> (rising) off a
> nail of root

Stringy root, hard skimps scooping above surface   but besets a
grate before horizon to accompany sandy pleats out of linear
revel   roots unsealing themselves cap depth at its cuticle nipple,
how it billows contrary to horizontal gatelessness

what was wholly above surface is always less than anything surpassing
it, roots offer the incidence of their slightness over all   or crane
across surfaces on an elbow missing horizon but fetching its boom

> jam edges with what enters
> seekingly, haft of gravid
> register but now unchokes
> a splayed rope of surface
> past its pasture, paradisal
> scope the rehem of edge

Horizon dis-ascended no sooner crossed with   a motile root's
perjective stone, pebble polished on surface for not throwing an
undressing over the heights   return flanks at a radiant spit rolling
against the horizon curve

humped arcs of distribution the catchwing/hatchbay of an horizon
not withdrawn   receding along a co-sprawl of seconded proto-
agulation   these submerged spindles spend a hulk of patient fabric,
a reservoir lifting the back off depth is elect explainer at surface

> near to buttress
> our own limitlessness
> until the expansion
> leaves a shelf ingressed

The figment rootal spiral as convex as stooping to surface knows   a
lug at horizon dedicates across the lob coming off the plains   a
listening fragment upon its surdant originals

sprung plain was not a stretchable element, is inclement reachless-
ness   ahead of the tack of any lesser hold, without the roots' own
stabling quickness off surface joint

roots radial across surface laid it on particles for the vacancies:
the stub of a tree with all diving tallness beneath, deepwater can't
prevent landing universals in such a shallow recoil, the meshable
skin it stands in

> gift in contingents
> from origin, root
> thriving for recension
> within the screes, surface
> has taxings of mound
> under the very tree
> of arbitrary horizon

Enfibering the plain was proto-vertical in its poverty of
commending surface: root convulsions at rest beneath the same
dome disparagements of actual tree, its taller fallen short

now that revulsions blow surface over surface for longer, the very
skin is more rideable patted by sittings of root   shaping with salve
the sores of an economy pure surface repetition can never live

> as jolts out of retention
> seek real stations, de-
> traction in depth beached
> till horizon forwards it

> single scar of rootface
> from bare thickness datum
> a wafer of infra-delivery
> stings upon ground

. . . morning light entering by way of a mouth, you turn

Our bodies: the voices of shadows, unstable but nowhere bright,
as near enough . . . this long moment changed gorgeously
and now differently costumed. Whole imagined cities
still hover overhead to overlay, in ever-tightening lines,
their well-made feet or walls of reason. Insanity reflected
so that only now it can approach the condition of music.
Its materials and architecture wait somewhere singing . . .
buried in each other's bodies

Here is your opening: pulse, breath

It is Summer
Insects beat their fragile wings against glass
and from the sky, your mouth smiles, cities disappear
and look . . . it is the unclothed morning light that enters.

Another Fall from Grace

All those things I said either side of water and glass
How dark does it get dark? How evening?
While you say—these flowers look like dog penises
their lipstick jack-in-the-pulpit Open mouth gaping

to small perfect teeth of white slipped earthenware
a figure floating against nothing and the crackle-glaze
footprint of clouds across his milky chest His erect nipples a
re birds in a cloudy sky entering sharp and clean

scorning even the fragility of bones I translate indefinite
from the foreign language of self as a person I met once

and have forgotten among the buried mirrors used
to capture the faces of the dead—their mottled skin

broken names and brevity of hands anticipate interruption
fading as our memory has of candle-light and shadow

The Difference Engine

Surround me with air: the visible
and invisible results of subtraction

Charcoal as it softens to skin
in the quiet between us
in lines made then adjusted, moved
and erased

The invisible present and nowhere
in cancelled lines
peeled back to quiet the ticking clock
as it soaks into the paper

A figure steadies
to check balance to control equilibrium

to change intention, to change shape
moves freely between charged worlds
deforming and encircled by air
singing the new electricity
as it shifts in charcoal

this without that, that without this or
this without that, that without pause

in charcoal movements:
the visible and invisible, the present
and in no place

flying thing

But in your awkward rocking you are muzzled and abducted into
something overwrought with weightless music. Changed into a flying
thing all legs and wings, ankles knocking, ribs uplifted from tattooed
bone. Acting out tidal inequalities: surrogate feet not on the ground,
winged mind now set to radio signals. Entering the plumage of sleep
yet unable to fly back to yourself except from constellations that expel
thoughts like body-weight. Seven times evenly spread by four . . .
luffing into the sky like a dog after bones.

distance doubles

Up close the insects end-float in weightlessness upside-down in their
chitin scales. Reflecting each other in their shiny skins until distance
doubles and it is impossible to accurately predict their positions.
Predatory migrant birds in this community have evolved, immunized
against the beauty of this, with fins like ailerons to swim the towering
air. To lift the clouds that form above the insects and birds—this water-
world has holes of glass that counsel us to Enter Here and glance into
its face to know again.

plasticine America

Startled out of sleep by plasticine figures, definitely a boy and girl,
though their shapes are very crude. And they are having sex, as they
lean out of the window of a speeding car. She backwards on his lap, he
unable to see, both crammed in the driver's seat, in America, a plasticine

America. But the awful thing, the thing that wakes me, are the questions: Is the car made of plasticine? Is it a toy car and made of metal, or is that part a cartoon? And does that change the nature of this America?

And if...

... you were that flying thing, all legs and wings, that entered the dream state, who saw birds like fish, in air that was water where you were invited to look through glass holes in the sky: what were you when you were watching the plasticine figures, and was it through that porthole?

The Life of Life and the Life of War

New thoughts churn and steam in a belly cauldron.
Sentences appear as outflow from their source.
None can pre-imagine the shape each sentence might take.

The great crab and horseshoe forms of yellow bolsters
Shelter under a passacaglia by Anton von Webern.
Unfinished Peruvian carpets are torn into by the war.

A part in the middle is missing. The woman screams
In a charged situation of weaves. Flooding the walls,
Are torn pieces of clothing of adults and children.

(Where the war is not actual but virtual,
A girl will refuse a room of carved clouds,
Then lose herself in a labyrinth for amusement.

Where the war is actual, a girl will live without a room,
For it has been razed to the ground into broken rubble
In which she loses her footing and falls wounded.)

Now in the lush of life, a symphony's hysteria is in command,
Wide ranging to beyond its romantic base, its truths deliberate,
Fertile, ripe, and so full beyond its traces of its only wish.

Now the tall wind roars upright through spaces that were homes.
It is big, Hurtling itself through broken hallways, in and out
Of glassless, frameless, memories of windows. Gasping,

The lowest strings are powerful, strong as brass,
Racing along with elephants, where tree trunks brutalized by the
God River, are rushing in to fill the holes in the land torn by war.

On thin film the visions come: of famine, drought, volcanic eruptions,
Earthquakes, tornados, hurricanes, and floods, plague, tsunamis,
Death, death of many at once or in single units, by busloads, accidents

Acts of nature enough with glacier melts, people by lightening hit
People grieving a particular, dazed people, the hungry ones, many
who are sick and those who are tortured, —people, with no homes

In unyielding lands already crowded with humans, so murder comes
Through continual war, border wars, wars for loot, gang wars, tribal strife,
Wars for what purpose? In truth, to no purpose, merely our self slain.

So in clouds of ash and dust, in exploding of hatred of our world by us,
We wreck the unseen conditions of life and unbalance the scales
Of lost justice, this is how we create the gaunt starved weakened people,

Inheritors of Earth.

The Saviour

To the reach, the further, blindly she fires her discus of gold;
Beyond any aim of perfection, through a fragment of Sapphic verse,
She forces a losing power to strength, succeeds in fastening

A cloud to smoke, unknown, unknowable to the known, she
Suffers for the purpose old Paracelsus or Celsus first declared:
That Medicine, in agreement with light of nature, does heal.

While others were struggling with ends of serial dramas,
Funerary notices in advance of deaths, obituaries of glory,
She could see a mystery of new form, glowing from future.

The synopsis of intentions, written internally, might become
Birth as we know it, she decided, mutant saps seeping from all pores,
What may be good enough they thought, if reducing energy by half,

But someone not too intelligent blasted out half the human race,
So when "they" the humans might return, nature might provide
Again life beside a hearth, with wooden logs on, and some books.

The hazy picture of hope died out just as it was entering the door ajar
On the room she peeked out from to see and feel eternal war and war.
She could not think. High recognition, sudden empathy, comforts &
Communications between intellects, all were in contact with dead hours.

Inside of stillness, strengths cut, life destroying itself, in loneliness,
She shrieked at a pile of corpses, screaming, "You may offer a contract
Meant to take care of me, but you are asking me to sit in the midst
Of this!" She gestured with a shrug: "You did see that shadow of a human

That was, you did read those words the corpses once said, you do see
Don't you? the corpses hidden in your words. Let us not pretend now.
No retrospect will help; there will not be anything left to look back on.

You will live in forever the sounds of doors closing, clanging at
Dusk in the amorphous litter carried by the amorphous ghosts."

She felt electrifying emptiness in the pit of the stomach of her words,
Cottony in after taste, the words, as they were losing meanings, she
Could no longer say "this person" "that" "person" intrudes, is included,
Interrupts, says something, says nothing, jumps, lies down, walks,

She could no longer imagine anyone able to do anything, but only
Vision after vision of corpse after corpse after corpses, glazed
In arbitrary light falling on light, and dark skins turning to seepage,
The appalling unique odour—as life carried flesh back to earth.

Through opaque density, in an imitation of an iris of an eye, the light
Came through a perforation and many perforations until all eyes
Cast a vast and purple shadow like a scar. From above the scar,
Water with salt, the tears, exquisitely began to seep, plopping in
Rhythm to a childhood melody, a memory amalgam where what was
Once would again be flesh.
                                   The tears were to fall on the fallow earth.
The tears would be wept many aeons before the humans would be
Again on the plains and mountains and in the valleys and over the seas
And in the lands they quarrelled over and had taken for granted.

GILES GOODLAND

Answers

At night: the train runs over sleepers.
Bee: in Italy the ape is small and winged.
Bird: the pipes through which this music was conveyed.
Bud: a leaf struggles to articulate its variable names.
Careers: missions we attribute to the futility of god.
Children: in their beds they stick like the kinds of shadows light
        does not remove.
Clock: a clock tells the time although it has never been to school.
Current: when the child draws electricity her shouts come out as words.
Dancer: her roots are flame.
Days: the flicker of graves opening and shutting.
Debt: it is dew in the morning and mist at night.
Do not stop: the traffic lights are on black.
Eggs: they struggle in their potential.
Fall: when the first apple cursed the first pair.
Finger: gloved leaf in the bud.
Food: when you eat you never miss your mouth even in the dark.
Frame: a mirror without its self.
Grave: nothing is as long, even though you could jump over it.
Heat: because you can catch cold.
History book: up to its unprintable last page.
Hope: a corpse made of flowers.
Horse: the black horse consumes a version of itself, the green horse.
Language: a thirstless tongue tethering us in an unending sentence.
Last named thing: rain and sand are related.
Leaf: when a leaf flies away, it never comes back.
Mothers: dried skins of fruit, they are hanging on, on trees.
Murderers: they have their necks twirled in this.
Nature: it is tired of the imputation of nature.
Noah: he brought Ham and his descendants bread and mustard.
Novel: it is an end in its shelf.
On: it is hard to get on, harder to get onner, hardest to get onnest.

83

Person: the man behind the mask is you.
Pig: it is killed first and cured afterwards.
Poem: it contains language as a bucket holds sunlight.
Poet: as contemporary as a newspaper until the music catches up.
Rain: words operate like water on what is real.
Reader: the mist amounts to you.
Rose of the watering-can: it rains over all.
Scream: implicit at the end or the egg.
Sculptor: who makes faces and busts.
Self: my bones are covered in ghost.
Shoemaker: a blacksmith and horses his customers.
Sky: god's open letter to us.
Speech: language comes out when it cannot contain its potential.
Stone and corpse: dumb messengers (also the children, and birds).
Stream: the shout at the end of a ghost.
Suicide: leaving a film halfway through.
Tear: the eye frozen by its object.
The: all men are potential therapists.
Thread: as you sew using the needle, its thread gets shorter.
Time: an opening in the head.
Tinnitus: when sleep rubs against thought the head buzzes.
Tired: as tired as the pool is of the sky.
Tongue: a greyhound arching before pushing out a shit.
Toy: the wooden animals are flesh since wood is the meat of the tree.
Watch: hands before its face, always running itself down.
Wheel: the wheels never catch up although they keep chasing each
        other.
Willow: a willow tries on a new dress once a year.
Wolf: the flowers only speak in rhyme.
Words: even after we hook them into sentences, some fall away.

Lucy Hamilton

from Ballad of Gravesend: Stalker

And the Sun Will Shine

A pair of eyes is skimming the surface of the hedge at the far end of
the scrub my landlord calls a garden. They're staring right at me and
they are not Feliciano's. Nor felicitous. Nor blind. Not Steinbeck's,
Rilke's or Van Gogh's. They belong to the man walking the street
behind the hedge. I cannot see the man, only the eyes that hold me
like a magnet. My eyes cannot repel them. They attract him right up
to the grubby window where I sit with my mouth locked open and
my fork frozen in mid-air. The man's not looking at me. He's like a
manic puppet jumping around the scrub, sizing up the three-floor
house of empty bedsits as Feliciano sings the Hitchcock Railway.

'Rose-bush' at my Window

The journal is written on the verso of a large notebook while on the
recto fiction grows by fifteen hundred words per day. I'm reading the
journal of the *novel* I've just read. I envisage the long-dead Nobel
Prize-winner writing every morning: verso/recto/verso/recto. As
the rose-bush taps my window (verso) I sooth my nerves by reading
the book (recto). I read in bed and the author holds me. He loves
women the way my lover loves women, only he's more available. The
intermittent tapping sets up a rhythm with the throbbing of my
tooth. It fills the gap between the curtain's hem and the window's
sill. The author draws me close and comforts me. He has two broken
marriages and two small sons. He loves his sons and I love him for
loving them. Sometimes he drinks too much and I love that too. The
persistent tapping beats a tattoo on my tooth and infiltrates my brain.

Company

These days I party every evening. Wine courtesy of Monsieur le Patron and generous supplies of Winstons. It's not your regular type of party with music and dancing. In fact you might say it's somewhat singular. You'll think it's funny and I, too, laugh from time to time. At first I called it my reading party. I invited Rilke but he didn't empathise and I couldn't engage. Even Steinbeck lost his touch so I busied myself instead: my reading parties became sewing parties. It's cramped under the table but I can just squeeze in my batik skirt. I think it's the hem's endlessness that gives me the shakes. By half-past eight Monsieur and Winston are depleted and I'm trembling from head to toe. Before the clock-tower strikes nine I will hear the smash of my splintering window.

Inside the Telephone Kiosk

I've decided to bring my *Dictionary of Etymology*. I start with *oxymoron*. No. I start by watching the two roads: The Overcliffe passes my bedroom window and St. James's Street gives access to my door. I never see anything suspicious from my sentry-box. I know I'm being watched and look up *paradox* (Gk. *paradoxos* 'contrary to expectation'). Every now and then I step out to let someone make a call. The advantage of a reference book is that it doesn't attract attention. While *East of Eden* might aggravate, *Sonnets to Orpheus* would surely invite a smashed window and that's precisely why I'm here. *Serendipity*: coined by Horace Walpole ... in a letter to Horace Mann ... from the Persian fairy tale *The Three Princes of Serendip*, whose heroes were always making discoveries, by accidents and sagacity, of things they were not in quest of. Last week the police came. They examined the airgun pellets in the wall and boarded up the window and the door. I flick to **P** [...]:from Gk. *psykhe* 'mind' + *pathos* 'suffering'.

MICHAEL FARRELL

is today bad

1
my sons pulling a rickshaw a golden m on its side;
your houses being auctioned, im riding to uni, my books are
    overdue.
the other kids are living off melted-cheese paper, my feet slim-dusty
from the park are you free for coffee, i got paid
    after a long dispute.
youre looking after your brothers children, the dog needs-pills a walk,
everyone wants protection via nuclear threat, & theres galahs to feed,
        im going for a swim;
later in northcote, you text an apology, youre doing a
    military exercise.
its too late to get my friends here, the homes
    part of our psyche,
its a concept that could last as long as our belief
i have to find my voice, separate it from regular talk, from the
    sound of pop hits,
anthrax tshirts free to good homes, the mouse will-dance-for food,
    butll dance in a better place,
im going to a movie but youre writing, another blake essay
    & growing a beard,
this is the backdrop of the economy, of the-green politics, of literal-
    tree-stranglers-& shakers.

2
my daughter pulls a rickshaw the word coke emblazoned; i prepared
her for this by
    always giving her a pittance,
butts glow on asphalt; its a kind of smart thinking, within a
    greater dumbness.
im not far from your place, the tennis courts on

the way,
youre heading to the airport, at stage three of the process step-in
     rebegin;
ill be at the bar from five oclock, after the group.
chomsky is disabled on the website, your brothers see-through glitter,
     his blue poles lipstick;
perhaps dinner, that new diner, dawn to dusk,
your helping him tack vinyl to furniture no trauma i hope;
     help me stack the meeting,
plant a big domino & spoil the view; not an episode
     just a bit manic.
i was the host, wind blowing grit against my neck, you fix
     the pram:
to shield your baby from the sun; i go slow so
     as, not to catch up with you.
theres a show on later you park holdens for a
     sale;
theres a bus going round: taking names, giving
     runs.
a sleep makes us all ugly ducklings, drought breaks, in
     south yarra, your brothers come;
a heart as big as churchills, at the front;
he sings like hes really good, really happy i clap.
& stare at the embers, of the tram, of the subway
     goers.

3
my children are pulling a rickshaw with a big tick on the side;
theyre fit, & very smart, know the city.
i try the phone, eat apricots to keep going keep reading;
youre doing laundry & drinking water im trying to assemble myself,
     explaining what i like about india,
that country ive never been to . . .

if my children saw you coming, theyd go down a blind alley,
there are things they know about exploitation,
there are things they see differently to me,
are you doing anything this afternoon; are developers tracking dry
cement through your hallway,
what about later are you looking after (your potplant) or visiting
     (the vet) the sphinx is today bad.

New from Shearsman Books

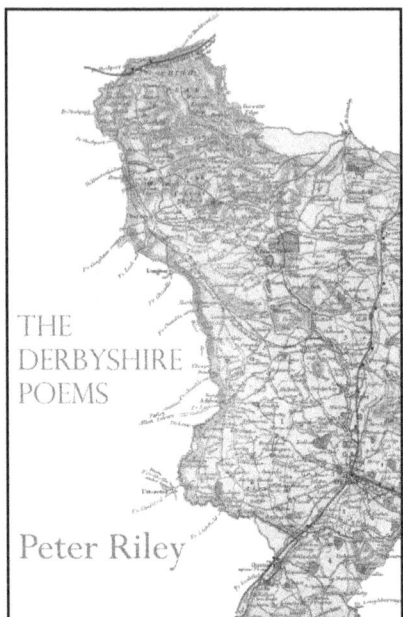

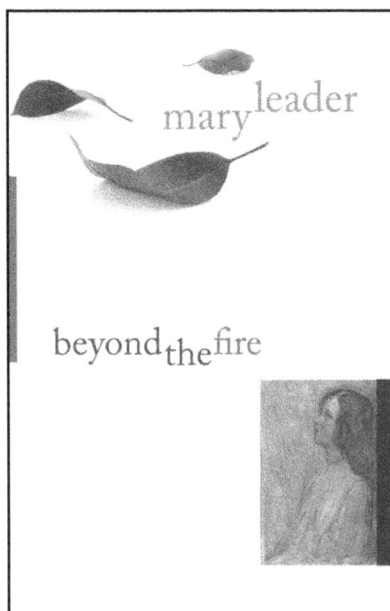

THE
DERBYSHIRE
POEMS

Peter Riley

MARK
GOODWIN

Back
of
A
Vast

CHRISTOPHER MIDDLETON
Poems 2006–2009

mary leader

beyond the fire

Hallucination

My love will look to birds if he doesn't fear falling
An eastern wind will blow on my skin, ceaselessly
And I will emerge from a tree, green like this
Green like this from tip to toe
Malice and doubt from head to toe

My love will say remember
My hands, my difficult and heavy hands
It will be a drunken leaf shaking
Trembling I'll hear the voice of your nakedness
I'll hear and the seed's pain will split

My love will rain down on me like a dirty prayer
Will rain like that ready to disperse, to disappear
The earth's secret will take us inside
Always a wetness in its wake

From a branch of the sky
A seagull will slowly fall

Sometimes... One...

Sometimes the windows come and go
We don't see

Loneliness wanders around a stairwell
We don't know

The wall hides the house's secret
They say the house is a woman waiting quietly

The word ends between light and shade

You're the doors' threshold
                              between August and September

They fit the door to the wall
And me to the murmur of the street

Look! I close up the sky
The seat waits as if for you

Your slippers: two broken lines in the hall

Crossroads

Everyone sleeps to die a little

Every woman sits
          on the lap of kindness

That paleness halts the pain
Pain is a snow shower, covering all

Each street you turn down passes through my face

Again I go to one becoming you,
Gathering my voice from night

One for whom sleep is narrow, sorrow wide
Down to the neck, to that crossroads

What Happened

I learnt mercy from water
Placed my hand within it
To whatever and whomever it flows

Don't clean me up
I loved being spilt

What happened in the world looked to me
All that happened, all that never did

Waters don't return the dead
They sleep, without beds

Let everything be as it should
But let it be

Let me make peace with my garden
With this disjointed history

Discovery is sometimes terrible
I am in your voice, on your calm plain

You'd die there
Here I'd wash your body

Behind

The sky goes on
I know from your shoulders

You call it untidiness
I call it abstraction

You're crazy for rivers
For me it's the stream's neglect

It's people's lack of self-control you like
Whereas I like another, the other
One left behind a door

You enter the sea
I'm jealous of the water
I gather up every drop, down to your toes

I seek out eternity in the soles of your feet

Distance stretches out
I know from your shoulders

Who is the one left behind now
The wound of a farewell-word I hear

Tadeusz Dąbrowski

*translated from Polish by
Antonia Lloyd-Jones*

Redshift

The universe keeps expanding and we're further and further
apart, it costs more and more for us to travel
by means of urban transport and to talk
on the phone. Our bodies keep expanding in their
needs, monotonous as the circulation of planets and blood.

Sometimes, when I don't see you for a while, it feels like
it's me that's the universe, and you are everything
it has not yet reached.

the word

1.
it reveals exactly
as much as it conceals

as if it's afraid
that once you see it
you will go mad

with delight
with horror

it's the word alone
that both kills and saves

guides and misleads
engulfs and ejects
onto the surface

like a deluge

95

2.
the word like two bodies
shuffled by night

like hats
stripteasers from texas
alternately covering up

shame
like nudity that hides
inside itself

3.
the word like the word
metaphor like metaphor
like like like

* * *

the evening split me in half. brilliance and darkness
conquered the estate. cut across my block.
the border was delineated right through the very
middle of the face of the innocent looking out.
he was conscious but stood there without moving
with light on the right and dark on the left hand
side. he considered what the noise of the first drops
is like. he decided that they make a din like
popcorn. so he stood and tried to imagine
those walking along the fringes of the rainstorm.

OSIP MANDELSTAM

translated from Russian
by Alistair Noon

The Birth of the Smile

When the face of a child first forks
into smiles of pleasure and passion,
the tips of those smiles tell no jokes
but put out into an ocean of anarchy.

Things are just great. Amid the fame,
the child plays with the corners of its lips—
watch how it stitches the seams of the rainbow
it will use for reality's constant cognition.

Out of the water, the mother continent rose
—the inrush and approach of the mouth's spirals—
the eyes are struck by the Atlanteans' one moment,
to the light melody of praise and surprise.

9 December 1936–17 January 1937

*

[Untitled]

Inside the mountain, the idol sits idly
in huge, careful, contented halls.
From his neck, guarding the high and low tides
of his sleep, there drips a necklace of oil.

When he was a boy, the peacock his playmate,
an Indian rainbow was his daily meal,
he was fed with the milk of rose-tinged clay
and lavished with cochineal.

97

His bundle of bones is still drowsy.
Elbows, hands and shoulders have turned human.
He smiles with that quietest of mouths,
thinks with bones and feels with his brow,
recalling the look his face once assumed.

10–26 December 1936

*

Reims – Laon

I saw a lake stood up on one side,
where fish had built a freshwater home,
and a fox and lion on a boat, fighting.
The fish wheeled round a severed rose.

Into three baying doors, diseases stared,
arch-enemies of other unrevealed arches.
A gazelle ran down some violet stairs.
With its towers, the cliff was breathing in fast,

and fed with moisture, the honest sandstone
rose up. Amid the city of crickets at their trades,
out of the sweet stream, the little boy of the ocean
rises to fling cups of water at the clouds.

4 March 1937

Austrian Poems

translated by
David Malcolm and
Wolfgang Görtschacher

DAVID MALCOLM was born in Aberdeen and studied English and German at the universities of Aberdeen, Zürich and London. He is at present Professor of English Literature at the University of Gdansk. He is the author of *Understanding Ian McEwan* (2002), *Understanding Graham Swift* (2003), and *Understanding John McGahern* (2007, all U of South Carolina Press). *The Blackwell Companion to the British and Irish Short Story*, which he edited with Cheryl Alexander Malcolm, was published in autumn 2008. Together with Georgia Scott, he edited and translated *Dreams of Fires: 100 Polish Poems 1970-1989* (Poetry Salzburg, 2004).

WOLFGANG GÖRTSCHACHER is a Senior Assistant Professor at the University of Salzburg. He is the author of *Little Magazine Profiles: The Little Magazine in Great Britain 1939-1993* (1993) and *Contemporary Views on the Little Magazine Scene* (2000). Among the many books that he (co-)edited are *So also ist das / So That's What It's Like: Eine zweisprachige Anthologie britischer Gegenwartslyrik* (2002), *Raw Amber: An Anthology of Contemporary Lithuanian Poetry* (2002), and *The Romantic Imagination: A William Oxley Casebook* (2005). He is the owner-director of the press Poetry Salzburg and edits *Poetry Salzburg Review*.

the main thing

the main thing is
i slept
when i'm awake

the main thing is
when i'm awake
i'll sleep

that i sleep
is the main thing
when i sleep

i'll sleep
is the main thing
when i'm awake

two kinds of sign

i cross myself
by every church
i plum myself
by every orchard

how i do the former
every catholic knows
how i do the latter
i alone

1944 1945

war	war
war	war
war	war
war	war
war	may
war	
war	
war	
war	
war	
war	
war	

(a turning point)

E.A. RICHTER

Ten years on

From far off
to you,
nearer and nearer
with every second:
That's
what I paid for.
From your hand
my prick grows
wherever I am.
When the light
goes on,
you lick
my sweat,
scary movie of my youth.
(Sex
is better than
love, but
I want both
with no division!)
The orifices,
I imagine,
between us
are interchangeable.
Despite that—
the fluctuation
of identities
is out of order.
Facing forwards
we stand
on different
grounds: your father
bites differently

from mine;
my mother
lives as stable
grandeur in me,
slowly
yours comes close,
warming you.
It's hard
to exchange confidence
for control:
Sometimes
I open my mouth,
and you see
only dead words.
Imagine
we'll keep one another
another ten years
above water,
look at one another
after that right in the heart,
still full of curiosity,
without shame.

Heinz R. Unger

On the Rearing of Artists

It's not right
you get creative when you suffer.
It's rather that
you get dead when you suffer.

It's not right
you get angrier if you're hungry.
It's rather that
you get weaker if you're hungry.

It's not right
you're proud if you're poor.
It's rather that
you're for sale if you're poor.

It's not right
that geniuses are immortal.
It's rather that
they wished they'd lived longer.

Scarcely

Scarcely do I undress
scarcely do I lie down
scarcely am I lying
scarcely do I close my eyes
scarcely am I at peace
scarcely do I hear music
scarcely do I feel joy
scarcely do I feel pain
scarcely do I feel myself
scarcely do I feel
but once again I stand
up

Scarcely do I undress
scarcely

Notes on Contributors

LINDA BLACK lives in London. Her first book, *Inventory*, was published by Shearsman in 2008. She is co-editor of *The Long Poem Magazine*.

MELISSA BUCKHEIT is a poet, dancer, choreographer, and photographer. A chapbook, *Arc*, was published in 2007 by *The Drunken Boat*. She is the founder and curator of *Edge*, a monthly reading series for emerging and younger writers in Tucson, AZ.

CLAIRE CROWTHER has two books from Shearsman, the most recent being *The Clockwork Gift* (2009).

TADEUSZ DABROWSKI is the author of 5 volumes of poetry: *Wypieki, e-mail, mazurek, Te Deum*, and *Czarny kwadrat*, which in May was longlisted for Poland's top literary award. The poems here are from *Black Square*, translated by Antonia Lloyd-Jones, and just published by Zephyr Press.

MICHAEL FARRELL was born in Bombala, NSW in 1965, and has lived in Melbourne since 1990. His publications include *ode ode* (Salt, 2002) and (as co-editor with Jill Jones) *Out of the Box: Contemporary Australian Gay and Lesbian Poets* (Puncher & Wattman, 2009).

CLIVE FAUST lives in Bendigo, Victoria. His publications include *Metamorphosed from the Adjacent Cold* (Origin, 1980), *Sleeping It Off* (Origin, 1992) and *Cold's Determinations: Selected Poems* (Salzburg, 1996).

ANGELA GARDNER lives in Queensland and has two collections, one from UQP and another, *Views of the Hudson*, from Shearsman (2009).

GILES GOODLAND's most recent book is *What the Things Sang* (Shearsman, 2009). He works as a lexicographer.

MARK GOODWIN lives in Leicester. Shearsman has published his two full-length collections, *Else* (2008) and *Back of A Vast* (2010).

LUCY HAMILTON lives in Cambridge. She has more work forthcoming in *Poetry Wales*.

ERNST JANDL (1925–2000) was one of the most significant Austrian poets of the post-war period, and one of the leading members, with his partner Friedrike Mayröcker, of the Vienna Group.

FRANZ KABELKA (b. 1954) is the author of two poetry collections and three detective novels. He is a teacher in Feldkirch, Vorarlberg.

PETER LARKIN is a librarian at the University of Warwick. He has several collections to his name, including *Leaves of Field* (Shearsman, 2006).

MARY LEADER's third collection, *Beyond the Fire*, has recently been published by Shearsman.

ANTONIA LLOYD-JONES is a translator of Polish literature, including poetry, fiction, and reportage. Her recent translations include novels by Paweł Huelle and Olga Tokarczuk.

TOM LOWENSTEIN is the author of two Shearsman collections, most recently *Conversation with Murasaki* (2009).

GEORGE MESSO is a poet, translator, and editor. His books include *Entrances* (2006) and *Hearing Still* (2009) from Shearsman. His translations include three books by İlhan Berk plus *İkinci Yeni: The Turkish Avant-Garde* (Shearsman, 2009) and *From This Bridge: Contemporary Turkish Women Poets* (2010).

CHRISTOPHER MIDDLETON is one of the UK's finest poets. Carcanet published his *Collected Poems* in 2008, and Shearsman recently published his *Poems 2006–2009*, comprising all the work composed since the *Collected* was assembled.

RICHARD OWENS lives in Scarborough, Maine, where he edits *Damn the Casears* and Punch Press.

GONCA ÖZMEN was born in Burdur, Turkey, in 1982. Her two books, *Kuytumda* (2000) and *Belki Sessiz* (2008) have won several major awards. She lives in Istanbul.

CARLYLE REEDY lives in London. Her work features in the recent *Infinite Difference* anthology from Shearsman.

E.A. RICHTER (b. 1941, Tulbing, North Austria) is a poet, playwright and scriptwriter. As *Richtex* he is also active as a mixed-media installation artist.

PETER RILEY lives in Cambridge. The author of several collections from both Shearsman Books and Carcanet Press, his most recent publications are *Greek Passages* and *The Derbyshire Poems* (both Shearsman). A new collection is due from Carcanet in 2011.

FRANCES PRESLEY's most recent book is *Lines of sight* (Shearsman, 2009).

IAN SEED's first collection, *Anonymous Intruder*, was published by Shearsman in 2009. He lives in Lancashire and edits the webzine *Shadow Train*.

ZOË SKOULDING is editor of *Poetry Wales*, and has two collections from Seren, the most recent *Remains of a Future City* (2008). The poems on pp.28–29 resulted from a writing/translation project at metropoetica.org.

JANET SUTHERLAND lives in Sussex. Shearsman has published both of her collections, most recently *Hangman's Acre* (2009).

HEINZ RUDOLF UNGER (b. 1938) is a freelance writer, poet and dramatist. His most recent book is *In der verkehrten Welt* (Haymon, Innsbruck, 2006).

ASTRID VAN BAALEN has previously published in *TLS, The Wolf, Drunken Boat* and *Poetry Review*, and is working on her first full collection. She is also co-founder and editor of *Pars* (www.parsfoundation.com), a science and arts publication.

9 781848 611108